ANGELS

ANGELS

Help from on High

Written and compiled by
Marianne Lorraine Trouvé, FSP

Pauline
BOOKS & MEDIA
Boston

Library of Congress Cataloging-in-Publication Data

Trouvé, Marianne Lorraine.

  Angels : help from on high / written and compiled by Marianne Lorraine Trouvé.

    p. cm.

  Includes bibliographical references (p. 129).

  ISBN 0-8198-0790-7 (pbk.)

  1. Angels--Christianity. 2. Catholic Church--Doctrines. 3. Catholic Church--Prayers and devotions. I. Title.

  BT966.3.T76 2010

  235'.3--dc22

2010018521

The Scripture quotations contained herein are from the *New Revised Standard Version Bible: Catholic Edition,* copyright © 1989, 1993, Division of Christian Education of the National Council of the Churches of Christ in the United States of America. Used by permission. All rights reserved.

Excerpts from the English translation of the *Catechism of the Catholic Church* for use in the United States of America, copyright © 1994, United States Catholic Conference, Inc. — Libreria Editrice Vaticana. Used with permission.

Special thanks to Lynn Geyer of ColorBlindMusic Ministries, Mt. Vernon, NY, for permission to reprint her angel story.

Cover design by Rosana Usselmann

Cover art: Gaudenzi Ferrari (1475–1546). Detail of Panels from an Altar-piece: The Annunciation: The Angel Gabriel, before 1511. © National Gallery, London /Art Ressource, NY.

Published by Pauline Books & Media, 50 Saint Pauls Avenue, Boston, MA 02130-3491

Printed in the U.S.A.

www.pauline.org

Pauline Books & Media is the publishing house of the Daughters of St. Paul, an international congregation of women religious serving the Church with the communications media.

4 5 6 7 8 9 10   20 19 18 17 16

Contents

Introduction

Angels have gotten some bad press. Artists often depict them as chubby babies with wings, flying lazily around clouds dotting a blue sky. But who would ever turn to such creatures for protection or help? Wouldn't that be like asking a two-year-old to balance your checkbook or change a flat tire? We can't *see* angels, and perhaps this is why artists often come up with the chubby babies. Consider instead this description of a mighty angel:

> And I saw another mighty angel coming down from heaven, wrapped in a cloud, with a rainbow over his head; his face was like the sun, and his legs like pillars of fire. He held a little scroll open in his hand. Setting his right foot on the sea and his left foot on the land, he gave a great shout, like a lion roaring. And when he shouted, the seven thunders sounded. (Rev 10:1–3)

Now that's an angel to reckon with! The imagery in the Book of Revelation is not meant to be taken literally. But it does help us realize that angels are mighty beings. Anyone who can snap the seven thunders to attention gets our respect. And God has given the angels to us as our helpers, protectors, and friends. They're on our side. They'll help us in all the difficulties that may creep into our lives. Their main job is to help us spiritually, but they also help us in all of life's problems. When the heat of temptation starts to burn, the angels come to our aid. When our relationships spin out of control like a jackknifed eighteen-wheeler, the angels come to our aid. When we have to mark another week of unemployment on the calendar, the angels come to our aid. No matter what upheavals we face, we can count on the angels.

But who are the angels? We can't see or hear them, because they don't have bodies like we do. They are neither male nor female. As completely spiritual beings, they are shrouded in mystery. But our faith lifts the veil and lets us peek in, at least a little.

The official Church teaching about the angels is actually quite limited. In the *Catechism of the Catholic Church*, apart from incidental references and summarizing articles, the major teachings about the angels are found in only fifteen out of a total of 2,865 articles—about two pages out of a two-inch-thick book. Yet over the centuries Christians have written many books and scholarly treatises about the angels. For example, the great medieval theologian and saint Thomas Aquinas devoted a large section of his *Summa Theologiae* to the angels. Much of what Saint Thomas wrote about the angels is theological speculation, but it makes for fascinating reading. (More on that later.)

Not only religious writers but also thinkers of all types have spent many hours pondering the angels. For example, in *The Angels and Us*, the philosopher Mortimer Adler recounts how he insisted that angels be included among the important ideas treated in the Great Books of the Western World series, which he edited.

For believers, though, angels are not ideas but persons and friends. In this book we'll get to know them better and deepen our friendship with them. We'll explore who and what angels are, what Scripture says about them, how they help us, and how the Church prays to them and with them. Along the way, we'll find out some interesting facts about the angels. This book also includes some true stories of people who believe they have been helped by an angel. While these accounts are not matters of faith, the testimonies show us the many ways that angels, like good coaches, help us in tough situations. All we need to do is ask them!

The Story of the Angels

Bless the LORD, O you his angels,
you mighty ones who do his bidding,
obedient to his spoken word.

— PSALM 103:20

What the Bible Teaches Us
About the Angels

If you open a Bible at random, chances are you won't have to read too far before you come across an angel. If you start at the beginning, you'll find the cherubim with the fiery sword guarding the way to the tree of life (see Gen 3:24). If you flip to the end, you'll find angels blowing trumpets, carrying prayers to heaven, and overseeing the "river of the water of life, bright as crystal, flowing from the throne of God and of the Lamb" (Rev 22:1). And angels are everywhere in between.

Filled with symbols and imagery, the Book of Revelation contains revelations given through the medium of angels. The visionary, John, is overwhelmed with all he has seen. It seems to him that the angels he sees were worthy of worship. The book tells us, "I, John, am the one who heard and saw these things. And when I heard and saw them, I fell down to worship at the feet of the angel who showed them to me; but he said to me, 'You must not do that! I am a fellow servant with you and your comrades the prophets, and with those who keep the words of this book. Worship God!'" (Rev 22:8–9). A few verses later the text adds, "Blessed are those who wash their robes, so that they will have the right to the tree of life and may enter the city by the gates" (Rev 22:14).

The first and last references to angels in the Bible have to do with the tree of life. This tree symbolizes the salvation God has prepared for us. As we walk the way of salvation, the angels are "fellow servants" who aid us along the way. Although the angels can help us with the material needs we have in this life, their main role is to help us spiritually and to guide us to salvation.

The vivid imagery found in the Bible can give us some idea of what angels are like, but these images describe something we can't see. Angels don't have wings, and they don't have bodies at all. They're entirely spiritual beings. It's hard to describe an invisible reality, which is why the Bible uses imagery. But the angels are very real even if they are invisible to our eyes.

That shouldn't surprise us. Even in the physical world we find natural forces that we cannot see but we know are real. How many of us know exactly what happens when we turn on a computer and are connected via the Internet with events happening around the world? How is it that electrical impulses beamed through space via satellite can bring such sharp images to our screens, whether a figure skater gliding on the ice, people digging out of rubble after an earthquake, or the pope presiding at a Mass? The geeks among us may know how it all happens. But I certainly don't.

If that is true for the ordinary things around us, how much more must it be true in the spiritual world God created. The angels are spiritual beings. While we can't fully understand them, we know by faith that they exist. The word "angel" actually means "messenger." The angels in Scripture carried out various missions that God sent them on. Based on that, Saint Augustine beautifully explained who and what the angels are: "'Angel' is the name of their office, not of their nature. If you seek the name of their nature, it is 'spirit'; if you seek the name of their office, it is 'angel': from what they are, 'spirit,' from what they do, 'angel'" (as quoted in the *Catechism of the Catholic Church*, no. 329).

The Testing of the Angels

The Bible doesn't tell us anything directly about the creation of the angels. But it does indicate that after their creation, God tested the angels in some mysterious way. Some of them failed the test. "Everyone who commits sin is a child of the devil; for the devil has been sinning from the beginning" (I Jn 3:8). When God created the angels, they had incredible gifts of nature and of grace. But they did not immediately enjoy the vision of God in heaven, for they had to freely choose to love God. He gave the angels free will, for he did not want to force his love on them. Instead, he offered it to them freely, in the hope that they would respond in love. We do not know exactly how the angels sinned, but some of them did sin, possibly by pride or envy. They freely chose to sin. God wanted them to love him and offered them the grace to do so. But they chose something less than God and rejected his love. Thus hell came into being.

The chief of these fallen angels is Satan, the adversary. He appears early in the story of salvation, in the guise of the serpent who tempted our first parents to sin against God (cf. Gen 3:1–15). Since then, Satan has never stopped tempting human beings. He even attempted to trip up and tempt Jesus himself! But "Jesus said to him, 'Away with you, Satan!'" (Mt 4:10). Jesus conquered Satan through the victory of the cross.

The Angels Can Help Us

The Bible narrates many stories showing how angels have always helped God's people. For example, when Abraham was about to sacrifice his son Isaac as God had commanded him, an angel intervened at the crucial moment. The angel told Abraham that God had only been testing him, and he should not harm his son (see Gen 22:1–14). When Jacob was traveling in a foreign land, he was reassured by a vision in which he saw a ladder going up to heaven, "and the angels of God were ascending and descending on it" (Gen 28:12). During the Exodus and its aftermath, when Moses led the people of Israel out of Egypt, the angels guided and protected them. God promised them: "I am going to send an angel in front of you, to guard you on the way and to bring you to the place that I have prepared. Be attentive to him and listen to his voice; do not rebel against him, for he will not pardon your transgression; for my name is in him" (Ex 23:20–21).

Many centuries have elapsed since Moses led his ragtag band through the desert. Under the guidance of the angels, they finally reached the Promised Land, the land flowing with milk and honey. As we go through the journey of our own lives, God still sends angels to guide us, just as he sent them to guide Moses and his people. They help us in our personal lives, and they also guide the whole People of God, the Church.

The *Catechism of the Catholic Church* (no. 332) sums up the many ways the angels have helped us:

> Angels have been present since creation and throughout the history of salvation, announcing this salvation from afar or near and serving the accomplishment of the divine plan: they closed the earthly paradise; protected Lot; saved Hagar and her child; stayed Abraham's hand; communicated the law by their ministry; led the People of God; announced births and callings; and assisted the prophets, just to cite a few examples.

While angels always guarded the People of God, they had a special role to play when Jesus came into the world, as we will see in the next section.

Jesus Christ and the Angels

The *Catechism of the Catholic Church* (no. 331) says that "Christ is the center of the angelic world." If you read through the Gospels looking for references to angels, you might be surprised to see how important they were to Jesus. The angels played a significant role in his life. The Gospels of Matthew and Luke have the most references to angels. While the angels aren't on every page, they appear at critical moments in Jesus' life.

The angels stepped in even before Jesus was born. Matthew relates how an angel appeared to Joseph in a dream and reassured him about Mary's pregnancy. This enabled him to go through with his marriage to Mary with a peaceful heart (see Mt 1:18–25). Luke's Gospel goes into great detail about the visit of the angel Gabriel to Zechariah, the father of John the Baptist, and to Mary. The annunciation to Mary has been a favorite Gospel scene, often depicted by Christian artists. Gabriel has a long conversation with Mary and invites her to become the mother of the Savior. One detail to notice is that the angel Gabriel gives Jesus his name: "And now, you will conceive in your womb and bear a son, and you will name him Jesus" (Lk 1:31). Luke reemphasizes that Gabriel named Jesus when he tells us about the circumcision: "he was called Jesus, the name given by the angel before he was conceived in the womb" (Lk 2:21).

The angels play a big part in the Christmas story. They appear to the shepherds and announce the good news that the Savior has been born:

> In that region there were shepherds living in the fields, keeping watch over their flock by night. Then an angel of the Lord stood before them, and the glory of the Lord shone around them, and they were terrified. But the angel said to them, "Do not be afraid; for see—I am bringing you good news of great joy for all the people: to you is born this day in the city of David a Savior, who is the Messiah, the Lord. This will be a sign for you: you will find a child wrapped in bands of cloth and lying in a manger." And suddenly there was with the angel a multitude of the heavenly host, praising God and saying,
>
> "Glory to God in the highest heaven,
> and on earth peace among those whom
> he favors!" (Lk 2:8–14)

Later, when Herod threatens the life of the infant Jesus, an angel appears to Joseph again and instructs him to flee to Egypt for safety. When Herod dies some years later, again an angel tells Joseph to take Jesus back to the land of Israel (see Mt 2:13–23).

During Jesus' public life, the Gospels have fewer references to the angels. Luke does mention that during Jesus' agony in the garden, an angel comes to comfort him: "Then an angel from heaven appeared to him and gave him strength" (Lk 22:43).

Angels appear again after Jesus' resurrection and ascension. The women who hurry to the tomb on Easter morning find an angel waiting for them: "Mary Magdalene and the other Mary went to see the tomb. And suddenly there was a great earthquake; for an angel of the Lord, descending from heaven, came and rolled back the stone and sat on it. His appearance was like lightning, and his clothing white as snow" (Mt 28:1–3). And when Jesus ascended to heaven, the dazed group of disciples saw two angels: "While he was going and they were gazing up toward heaven, suddenly two men in white robes stood by them. They said, 'Men of Galilee, why do you stand looking up toward heaven? This Jesus, who has been taken up from you into heaven, will come in the same way as you saw him go into heaven'" (Acts 1:10–11).

When Jesus talks about angels in the Gospels, he's usually referring to the final judgment and his coming again in glory. The angels will have an important role to play at that time. They will "reap the harvest," as it were, separating the good and the bad: "The Son of Man will send his angels, and they will collect out of his kingdom all causes of sin and all evildoers" (Mt 13:41). Jesus mentions this scene of his second coming several times. Later in Matthew's Gospel, when Jesus depicts the great scene of the final judgment, he says, "When the Son of Man comes in his glory, and all the angels with him, then he will sit on the throne of his glory" (Mt 25:31).

With angels doing all these mighty deeds, it's no wonder that sometimes Christians have gotten a little too carried away, almost to the point of worshiping the angels along with Christ. This even happened in the early Church. In his letter to the Colossians, Saint Paul addresses this issue. He warns against getting swept up into angel worship. He insists that Jesus Christ alone is the one whom we worship, not the angels. Paul writes, "Do not let anyone disqualify you, insisting on self-abasement and worship of angels" (Col 2:18). So we certainly should never worship angels. They are creatures, and, like us, they worship God. Although we don't go to the extreme of worshiping angels, we can still recognize their power and ability to help us and ask them to aid us on our journey to God.

Three Familiar Angels:
Michael, Raphael, Gabriel

Are not all angels spirits in the divine service,
sent to serve for the sake of those
who are to inherit salvation?

— Hebrews 1:14

Why Three Angels?

Interest in angels crops up in unexpected places. Not long ago I was in a store and a man came up to me and asked, "What angels are named in the Bible?" Although the Bible mentions angels often, it names only three of them: Michael, Gabriel, and Raphael. After that incident I started to wonder why only those three angels are named. Biblical names are important because they express something about the person. They also often say something about the special work God calls them to. As I pondered this, an idea came to mind that might offer some light about why three and only three angels are named in the Bible.

This idea flows from what can be called "Way, Truth, and Life" spirituality. This is based on what Jesus says about himself at the Last Supper: "I am the way, and the truth, and the life. No one comes to the Father except through me" (Jn 14:6). The founder of the Daughters of Saint Paul and the whole Pauline Family, Blessed James Alberione, made this idea the cornerstone of his spirituality.

Much could be said about it. But to condense it a bit, Jesus' definition of himself as Way, Truth, and Life concisely expresses how he makes us holy. Holiness involves the complete person—mind, will, and heart. Jesus himself is the Truth that enlightens our mind; he is the Way we must follow; and he is the Life who raises us to the life of grace with him.

The aspect of Truth speaks especially to the human quest for meaning. What is the purpose of life? Why am I here and where am I headed? These are the most profound questions that human beings can ask, and people have always pondered them. In the Gospel we find Jesus, the "true light, which enlightens everyone" (Jn 1:9). As Pope John Paul II said so often, Jesus is the one who reveals us to ourselves. In Jesus the Truth, our minds find the fullness of truth.

The aspect of the Way brings us into the area of how to live a fully human life. Knowing the truth is vital but not enough. Unless it is translated into action, it could remain sterile, like a bookshelf crammed with unread books. As the Way, Jesus shows us how to live a fully human life. Ultimately, this is the way of love. The secret of finding happiness is to pour ourselves out in a loving gift of self.

This may lead to suffering, as Jesus himself experienced as he hung dying on the cross. But resurrection follows. In Jesus the Way, our wills find the strength of virtue.

The aspect of Life leads us to the fullness of grace and the spiritual life. Through prayer, the sacraments, and the Word of God, Jesus nourishes us and fills us more and more with his divine life. As this life takes root in our souls and grows, our whole lives are transformed into a hymn of praise to God. In Jesus the Life, our hearts find the fullness of grace and love.

So how is all this related to the angels? The three angels—Michael, Gabriel, and Raphael—can be seen as part of the Way, Truth, and Life spirituality. Michael, who stood for God and overcame the devil and his angels, leads us along the *way* of virtue. Gabriel announced the Good News, the *truth* of the Gospel. And Raphael, the angel who brought healing to the family of Tobit, can be seen as representing the fullness of *life* that God desires for us. So we can find in these three angels a good summary of the Christian life. Perhaps the names of only three angels were revealed because the three of them together express in some way what Jesus meant by the Way, the Truth, and the Life.

Saint Michael: Our Protector
and Helper on the Way to God

"At that time Michael, the great prince, the protector of your people, shall arise" (Dan 12:1).

On a rocky island off the coast of Normandy in France, a huge Benedictine monastery rises spectacularly into the air. Although receding tides leave it connected to the mainland, the water rushes back in at great speeds as the tide turns. These treacherous currents and the quicksands in the area have challenged pilgrims for centuries—pilgrims on their way to Saint Michael's greatest shrine: Mont Saint-Michel. Around the year 708, Bishop Aubert of the diocese of Avranches reportedly had a vision of Saint Michael. The angel asked the bishop to build a church in his honor on the rocky island in the Atlantic. Aubert built the shrine, which in 966 became a Benedictine monastery. Devotion to Saint Michael flourished there and drew pilgrims from all over Europe. During the French Revolution the shrine was converted to a prison; then, in 1874, it became a public monument. In 1922, however, the French government allowed it to be used as a place of worship again.

The rugged terrain of Mont Saint-Michel is an appropriate setting for a tough angel often invoked for help in the struggles of life. Saint Michael is the best-known angel, and devotion to him has flourished through the centuries. Many parish churches claim him as their patron. Michael is also known as one of the saints who spoke to Saint Joan of Arc to encourage her in her unique mission from God. But in a particular way, Michael helps us in the spiritual battle against temptation and sin. This derives mainly from a text in the Book of Revelation:

> And war broke out in heaven; Michael and his angels fought against the dragon. The dragon and his angels fought back, but they were defeated, and there was no longer any place for them in heaven. The great dragon was thrown down, that ancient serpent, who is called the devil and Satan, the deceiver of the whole world—he was thrown down to the earth, and his angels were thrown down with him. (Rev 12:7–9)

This text indicates that in some way Satan rebelled against God at the dawn of time before human life on earth existed. Christian tradition has found in this text a basis for Michael's key role in the battle against evil and Satan, a spiritual battle. Because Scripture presents Michael as the protector of God's People, he is seen as the adversary of Satan.

The Bible also refers to the Archangel Michael in a few other passages that deal with the end times. These Scripture passages form the basis for devotion to the Archangel Michael. The Book of Daniel states: "At that time Michael, the great prince, the protector of your people, shall arise" (Dan 12:1; see also 10:13). The Letter of Jude also refers to Michael contending with the devil (v. 9). Apocalyptic writing is difficult to interpret and need not be taken literally. However, it indicates that Michael has a special role in protecting us from evil and dangers, especially spiritual dangers. In speaking of the fall of the angels, the *Catechism of the Catholic Church* states: "We find a reflection of that rebellion in the tempter's words to our first parents: 'You will be like God'" (no. 392). Michael, instead, chose to worship and adore God alone. The very name "Michael" means "Who is like God?"

Michael, then, can be seen as a leader who shows us the way to God and helps us along the path of virtue. That is also why he has also been often invoked as a patron to help us in the hour of death. At that decisive moment, when we might be tempted to doubt God's mercy, Michael steps in to encourage us. Christian art has often depicted him holding the scales of justice as souls are brought

before God to be judged. As our advocate and protector, Michael intercedes to obtain God's mercy.

Toward the end of the nineteenth century, Pope
Leo XIII decreed that the prayer to Saint Michael
be recited by all the faithful at the end of the Mass.
Although this practice was discontinued in many
places with the renewal of the liturgy after the
Second Vatican Council, we can still pray privately
for Saint Michael's help in overcoming evil. This
great archangel will help us to resist temptation,
avoid sin, and do good. He leads us along the way
of virtue.

Saint Michael is invoked as a special protector
of the Church against the power of Satan. Michael
is also the patron of soldiers, mariners, radiologists,
and police officers.

Saint Gabriel:
The Messenger of the Gospel

*"I am Gabriel. I stand in the presence of God, and I have been
sent to speak to you and to bring you this good news" (Lk
1:19).*

If Michael can be seen as the angel who leads
us on the way to God, Gabriel can be seen as the

angel who teaches us about the truth of God. He can help us see into spiritual realities more deeply and understand them better. The name "Gabriel" means "strength of God." In the Gospel, Jesus speaks of those who accept God's word, comparing them to a person who builds a house on rock. Because of the strength of their foundation, they will not be shaken when life's trials threaten to overwhelm them. Like a rock that is unmoved as floodwaters crash over it, those who center their lives on God's word are strong.

Gabriel's role as a teacher is brought out in the various appearances he makes in the Bible. The first place he appears is in the Book of Daniel. The young Daniel has received a series of visions from God, which he finds hard to understand. This part of the Book of Daniel is written in an apocalyptic style. Its symbolism and imagery are not meant to be taken literally. Exactly what the visions were referring to is less important for our discussion than that the text brings in an angel to act as an interpreter and guide—and that angel is Gabriel. He is sent to help Daniel understand what he was seeing:

> When I, Daniel, had seen the vision, I tried to understand it. Then someone appeared stand-

ing before me, having the appearance of a man, and I heard a human voice by the [River] Ulai, calling, "Gabriel, help this man understand the vision." So he came near where I stood; and when he came, I became frightened and fell prostrate. But he said to me, "Understand, O mortal, that the vision is for the time of the end." (Dan 8:15–17)

A few verses later, chapter 9 begins with Daniel pleading with the Lord for an understanding of the Scriptures (it has to do with some teachings from the prophet Jeremiah). Daniel does penance by fasting in order to receive divine light: "Then I turned to the LORD God, to seek an answer by prayer and supplication with fasting and sackcloth and ashes" (Dan 9:3). After Daniel beseeches God with a long and fervent prayer, the answer comes to him through the Archangel Gabriel:

While I was speaking, and was praying and confessing my sin and the sin of my people Israel, and presenting my supplication before the LORD my God on behalf of the holy mountain of my God—while I was speaking in prayer, the man Gabriel, whom I had seen before in a vision, came to me in swift flight at the time of the evening sacrifice. He came and said to me, "Daniel, I have now come out to give you wisdom and understanding. At the beginning of your supplications a word went out, and I have come to declare it, for you are greatly beloved. So consider the word and understand the vision." (Dan 9:20–23)

Then the book tells us how Gabriel explains to Daniel the meaning of what he has seen in his visions. It's clear that Gabriel's role is to teach, to impart wisdom and knowledge. He is a great communicator, and that is why Gabriel is venerated as the patron of those who use the communications media in all its various forms. Using the model of Way, Truth, and Life, Gabriel is a teacher of the truth that leads us to God.

Gabriel's role of teaching and leading us along the path of truth continues in the New Testament. The Gospel of Luke tells us that Gabriel was the angel who was sent to Zechariah and to Mary to announce the births of John the Baptist and of Jesus. Luke places these two dramatic episodes side by side in the first chapter of his Gospel. Gabriel received two different responses, and we can learn from them both. Zechariah was a priest married to Elizabeth, Mary's kinswoman. Zechariah and Elizabeth had not been able to have children, and they were now past the age for it. One day Zechariah was serving in the temple while the people were praying outside:

> Then there appeared to him an angel of the Lord, standing at the right side of the altar of incense. When Zechariah saw him, he was terrified; and fear overwhelmed him. But the angel said to him, "Do not be afraid, Zechariah, for your prayer has been heard. Your wife, Elizabeth, will bear you a son, and you will name him John. You will have joy and gladness, and many will rejoice at his birth, for he will be great in the sight of the Lord. He must never drink wine or strong drink; even before his birth he will be filled with the Holy Spirit. He will turn many of the people of Israel to the Lord their God. With the spirit and power of Elijah he will go before him, to turn the hearts of parents to their children, and the disobedient to the wisdom of the righteous, to make ready a people prepared for the Lord." Zechariah said to the angel, "How will I know that this is so? For I am an old man, and my wife is getting on in years." The angel replied, "I am Gabriel. I stand in the presence of God, and I have been sent to speak to you and to bring you this good news. But now, because you did not believe my words, which will be fulfilled in their time, you will

become mute, unable to speak, until the day these things occur." Meanwhile the people were waiting for Zechariah, and wondered at his delay in the sanctuary. When he did come out, he could not speak to them, and they realized that he had seen a vision in the sanctuary. He kept motioning to them and remained unable to speak. When his time of service was ended, he went to his home. After those days his wife Elizabeth conceived, and for five months she remained in seclusion. She said, "This is what the Lord has done for me when he looked favorably on me and took away the disgrace I have endured among my people." (Lk 1:11–25)

Gabriel certainly appears as a no-nonsense type of angel. He expects that a priest would believe him, and when Zechariah doubts his words, Gabriel gives him an appropriate sign. In one way, it is a bit ironic that the angel we venerate as the patron of communicators makes Zechariah unable to speak for at least nine months. But perhaps it's a way of telling us that we also need silence in order to communicate. If Zechariah couldn't speak, he could still ponder, and he must have used the time to grow in his understanding of the ways of God.

This incident with Zechariah also gives Gabriel the opportunity to explain a bit more about who he is. He stands in the presence of God. The Book of Revelation speaks of seven angels who evidently have a special role of service: "And I saw the seven angels who stand before God, and seven trumpets were given to them" (Rev 8:2). It's not clear whether Gabriel is meant to be included in the group of seven angels in Revelation, but in any case he definitely plays an important role in the history of salvation. Luke then tells us about the most important event in that history.

Gabriel is sent to Mary, a virgin who lived in the little town of Nazareth. What the angel would propose to Mary would change the entire history of the world:

> In the sixth month the angel Gabriel was sent by God to a town in Galilee called Nazareth, to a virgin engaged to a man whose name was Joseph, of the house of David. The virgin's name was Mary. And he came to her and said, "Greetings, favored one! The Lord is with you." But she was much perplexed by his words and pondered what sort of greeting this might be. The angel said to her, "Do not be afraid, Mary, for you have found favor with God. And now, you will conceive in your womb and bear a son, and you will name him Jesus. He will be great, and will be called the Son of the Most High,

and the Lord God will give to him the throne of his ancestor David. He will reign over the house of Jacob for ever, and of his kingdom there will be no end." Mary said to the angel, "How can this be, since I am a virgin?" The angel said to her, "The Holy Spirit will come upon you, and the power of the Most High will overshadow you; therefore the child to be born will be holy; he will be called Son of God. And now, your relative Elizabeth in her old age has also conceived a son; and this is the sixth month for her who was said to be barren. For nothing will be impossible with God." Then Mary said, "Here am I, the servant of the Lord; let it be with me according to your word." Then the angel departed from her. (Lk 1:26–38)

In a very real way, the Archangel Gabriel was the first evangelizer. How is that so? An evangelizer is someone who brings the Good News about Jesus Christ to others. After Gabriel greeted Mary, Luke tells us that Mary "was much perplexed by his [Gabriel's] words and pondered what sort of greeting this might be" (Lk 1:29). Mary is deeply troubled, so she asks: "How can this be, since I know not man?" Then Gabriel explains: "The Holy Spirit will come upon you and the power of the Most High will overshadow you; therefore the child to be born will be holy; he will be called Son of God."

These words that Gabriel used about Jesus are the words that the early Church used to proclaim the Gospel in light of its Easter faith, that is, what the Church came to believe about Jesus because of his resurrection. Gabriel's words actually reflect a standard formula that was used in early Christian preaching about Jesus. Scripture scholars have shown this by comparing this text to others. For example, a similar text is found in Saint Paul's Letter to the Romans, where he speaks of "the gospel concerning his Son, who was descended from David according to the flesh and was declared to be Son of God with power" (Rom 1:3–4). Scholars tell us that by using this formula, Luke's text shows that Gabriel was actually proclaiming the Gospel to Mary. So we can truly say that Gabriel was an evangelizer. And Mary was the first person to hear the Gospel.[1]

And how did Mary respond? Once she clearly understood what God was asking of her, Mary responded with faith. She immediately offered herself to the Lord. She wanted to cooperate with her whole being, her entire self. Mary's reply, "Let it be done unto me," expresses not just a half-hearted

1. See R. E. Brown et al., *Mary in the New Testament* (Philadelphia: Fortress Press, 1978), 115–119.

"all right," but a wholehearted, "Yes, Lord! I want to do this. Send me!" Luke's text itself indicates this, for he uses a verb form that expresses an enthusiastic willingness, a readiness for action. Mary's acceptance shows us the joy of giving ourselves wholeheartedly to God.[2]

Mary's yes at the annunciation was a different kind of yes from the one Jesus said to his Father during the agony in the Garden of Gethsemane. That was a yes said amid great suffering. Days of suffering come into all our lives. And Mary, too, said another yes, a painful yes, as she stood at the foot of the cross on Calvary. Throughout our whole Christian life, joys and sorrows mingle. The angel's words and Mary's example at the annunciation remind us that at the very deepest level, we can find happiness by accepting and acting on God's word. Mother Thecla Merlo, the cofounder of the Daughters of Saint Paul, put it well when she said, "Even if you cannot always be joyful, you can always be at peace."

---

2. See Ignace de la Potterie, *Mary in the Mystery of the Covenant* (New York: Alba House, 1992), 35.

Saint Raphael: The Angel of Healing

"I am Raphael, one of the seven angels who stand ready and enter before the glory of the LORD" (Tob 12:15).

The third angel Scripture tells us more about is Saint Raphael, whose name means "God heals." As we continue to look at the angels through the prism of Way, Truth, and Life, Raphael stands out as the angel who leads us to the abundance of life. His story is found in the delightful Book of Tobit.[3]

Tobit was not written as an historical account but as an edifying story that teaches important moral lessons. It is closely related to the wisdom literature in the Bible. It is significant because the book teaches us about the role the angels play in our lives.

The story revolves around three people in particular: an old man named Tobit; his son, Tobias; and their relative, Sarah. Tobit is a devout Jew living in Nineveh, the Assyrian city to which the people of Israel were carried off in exile. He spends his life

---

3. This book is one of the "deutero-canonical" books of the Bible. This simply means that the Catholic Church accepts it as authentic Scripture inspired by God. However, not all Christian churches accept it as part of the Bible.

doing good deeds such as burying the dead, but other people ridicule him for this. As the story unfolds, one hot night he goes outside to try and sleep, and some bird droppings fall into his eyes, causing cataracts. He becomes blind, and he grows despondent over his situation. He prays to God for deliverance.

Meanwhile, his relative Sarah, who lives in another city, is having her own troubles. She has been married seven times, but each of her husbands was killed on his wedding night by an evil demon named Asmodeus. She is at the point of despair and has even contemplated suicide. But she resists that temptation and turns to God in prayer. The book tells us: "At that very moment, the prayers of both of them were heard in the glorious presence of God. So Raphael was sent to heal both of them" (Tob 3:16–17).

This is the point of the story: that God sends the angels to help us in our difficulties. The rest of the story of Tobit gives the details of how God worked it all out through the angel's ministry.

Tobit decides to send his son, Tobias, on a journey to collect a debt someone owes. "So Tobias went out to look for a man to go with him to Media, someone who was acquainted with the way. He went out and found the angel Raphael standing in front of him; but he did not perceive that he was an angel of God" (Tob 5:4). Tobit wants to meet the man who would accompany his son, so Tobias brings in Raphael to meet him. When he does, Tobit can't help but let his bitterness slip out:

> "What joy is left for me any more? I am a man without eyesight; I cannot see the light of heaven, but I lie in darkness like the dead who no longer see the light. Although still alive, I am among the dead. I hear people but I cannot see them." But the young man [Raphael] said, "Take courage; the time is near for God to heal you; take courage." (Tob 5:10)

Raphael accompanies Tobias on the journey. Along the way, Tobias stops to bathe in a river, and a large fish attacks him. Under the angel's instructions, Tobias grapples with the fish in the water, captures it, and cuts out its heart, liver, and gall to use for medicine.

Tobias still doesn't realize that Raphael is an angel. As the rest of the story plays out, Tobias ends up marrying Sarah. Through his prayers and the help of the angel, he avoids the fate of Sarah's first seven husbands. He returns home with his new wife, and Raphael tells Tobias how to heal his father of cataracts, using the medicine made from the fish. The angel finally reveals his identity:

I will now declare the whole truth to you and will conceal nothing from you. Already I have declared it to you when I said, "It is good to conceal the secret of a king, but to reveal with due honor the works of God." So now when you and Sarah prayed, it was I who brought and read the record of your prayer before the glory of the LORD, and likewise whenever you would bury the dead. And that time when you did not hesitate to get up and leave your dinner to go and bury the dead, I was sent to you to test you. And at the same time God sent me to heal you and Sarah your daughter-in-law. I am Raphael, one of the seven angels who stand ready and enter before the glory of the LORD." (Tob 12:11–15)

As the angel of healing, Raphael's mission is to lead us to the fullness of life. While this can and does include physical healing, the ultimate goal is the health of our spiritual life. The Archangel Raphael is regarded as the angel of joy and is invoked as the angel of healing, the patron of travelers and bearers of the Good News, and the patron of men and women seeking a good spouse. When we turn to him in prayer, Raphael will lead us along the way to God.

The feast of all three angels, Michael, Gabriel, and Raphael, is celebrated on September 29. Since the sixth century, the Church has celebrated the feast of Saint Michael on that date. It recalls the dedication of the ancient Basilica of Saint Michael the Archangel, located northeast of Rome. The feast, often called "Michaelmas," was popular throughout the Middle Ages and was celebrated with great solemnity. The new Roman calendar that took effect after Vatican II added Saint Raphael and Saint Gabriel to the celebration so all three angels would be honored together.

Guardian Angels

For he will command his angels concerning you
to guard you in all your ways.

— PSALM 91:11

Our Life Coaches

Would you like to have a personal life coach—for free? Someone who stands in your court, cheers you on, keeps you on course, and pushes you when you feel like dropping out? Every great athlete has a coach. No matter how much raw talent a person has, it needs to be shaped. What's true for sports is even truer for the other aspects of life. Like a potter who forms clay into a beautiful vase, a good life coach helps shape a person's life into a work of art. The coach will help the person find direction, set up goals, and figure out ways to reach those goals.

The need for a coach is even greater in our spiritual lives. We make choices all the time—about family and friends, work and careers, and, most importantly, our relationship with God. Life is made of all the things we do each day, and all of them have an impact on our spiritual lives. Our guardian angels can guide us in success, and encourage us when we're discouraged. As we go through our day-to-day lives, the angels stay at our side no matter what happens.

The guardian angels are our life coaches. They help us find our way through the mazes of our life on earth. Each of us has a different maze to get through. God has given us angels to coach us along the way, always with an eye on the ultimate goal. The coach will help us figure out which paths will lead us to happiness and peace of mind here on earth, and to eternal life with God forever.

Where did we get the idea that people actually have guardian angels? Ultimately it comes from Scripture. In the Old Testament we find God sending angels to protect and guard the whole people of Israel. For example, during the Exodus, as Moses leads the people out of Egypt, God gives him some instructions and commands. Then God makes a promise: "I am going to send an angel in front of you, to guard you on the way and to bring you to the place that I have prepared. Be attentive to him and listen to his voice" (Ex 23:20–21).

The angel is sent to guard the *whole* people. In Biblical times, the emphasis was more on the group than the individual. With the modern emphasis on individuals and their rights, we may not think as much about the well-being of the whole group. But it is reasonable to suppose that some angels guard groups and nations. Before the Blessed Mother appeared to the three children at Fatima, an angel appeared to them to prepare them for Mary's visit. The angel identified himself as the guardian angel of Portugal.

The Bible contains many references to the way angels surround and protect us. We find in the Psalms, for example, "The angel of the LORD encamps around those who fear him, and delivers them" (Ps 34:7), and "For he will command his angels concerning you to guard you in all your ways" (Ps 91:11). And Jesus said, "Take care that you do not despise one of these little ones; for, I tell you, in heaven their angels continually see the face of my Father in heaven" (Mt 18:10).

Quoting Saint Basil on the angels, the *Catechism of the Catholic Church* states:

> From infancy to death human life is surrounded by their watchful care and intercession. "Beside each believer stands an angel as protector and shepherd leading him to life." Already here on earth the Christian life shares by faith in the blessed company of angels and men united in God. (no. 336)

In the quote above, Saint Basil is referring to eternal life. Our angels, of course, can and often do protect us from hazards we meet in our life here on earth. But their major concern is the life of the spirit. Usually we aren't aware of the ways in which our angel helps us. But sometimes God allows them to manifest themselves to certain persons. One woman who often was able to see and talk with her guardian angel was Saint Gemma Galgani. She lived in Italy in the latter part of the nineteenth century, dying in 1903 at the age of twenty-five. In a letter to her spiritual director, Gemma explained how her angel helped her along the path of holiness, just as a coach would guide an athlete. The angel's main concern was that Gemma become a little holier every day. The angel suggested ways that she could change her life. She told her director that the angel looked at her with affection and gave her peace of heart. While the way Gemma interacted with her angel was extraordinary, each one of our guardian angels also wants to bring us peace of heart.

The Angel of Peace

In fact, from ancient times the angel as protector has been called the "angel of peace." This term was found in ancient Hebrew literature, and then in Christian writings. Saint Basil wrote about some persons he had sent on a trip, "with a prayer to our loving God to give them an angel of peace to help and accompany them."[4]

The angel of peace inspires us to act in such a way that we will have peace of heart. What does that mean on a practical level? The angels know that we never find peace when we act contrary to the will of God. So they guide us away from sin and toward leading a holy life. Sometimes their influence can be subtle. While we can experience temptations toward sin, the angels instead give us inspirations to do good.

Good coaches know how important it is to keep an athlete focused on the positive. They even use visualization techniques to prepare for the big moment on the field. Angels can help us in the same way. Not every thought that comes into our minds is inspired by an angel. That's where discernment comes in. But they often do send us positive thoughts. Because they're subtle, it's easy to ignore them or not even notice. But how different life would be if we paid attention to those urgings to do good and followed through on them!

---

4. Saint Basil, Letter II, http://www.ccel.org/ccel/schaff/npnf 208.ix.xii.html.

The Angel of Repentance

The guardian angel is also the angel of repentance. In this capacity, the angel leads us to inner conversion of heart and a turning away from sin. Angels guide and correct us, and restore us to spiritual health if we have lost it. Jesus himself indicates that the angels have this role when he said, "Just so, I tell you, there is joy in the presence of the angels of God over one sinner who repents" (Lk 15:10).

The idea that angels guide us to repentance was the theme of a second-century work called *The Shepherd of Hermas*. This allegorical book featured an "angel of repentance" who took the form of a shepherd. Throughout the book, the angel gives commands and advice on how to live a good Christian life. The angel sums up the message:

> All these things which are written above I, the shepherd, the angel of repentance, have declared and spoken to the servants of God. If then ye shall believe and hear my words, and walk in them, and amend your ways, ye shall be able to live. But if ye continue in wickedness and in bearing malice, no one of this kind shall live unto God.[5]

---

5. *Shepherd of Hermas* 33[110]:1. http://wesley.nnu.edu/biblical_studies/noncanon/fathers/ante-nic/hermas1.htm.

The Angel of Prayer

The third role of the guardian angel is to be an angel of prayer, that is, the angel who presents our prayers to God. This role is pictured vividly in the symbolism of the Book of Revelation:

> Another angel with a golden censer came and stood at the altar; he was given a great quantity of incense to offer with the prayers of all the saints on the golden altar that is before the throne. And the smoke of the incense, with the prayers of the saints, rose before God from the hand of the angel. (Rev 8:3–4)

In some way the angels assist us as we pray, helping us as we offer worship to God. Origen, an ancient writer famous for his teachings on Scripture, wrote that "beholding ever the face of the Father in heaven and looking on the Godhead of our Creator, the angel of each person, even of 'little ones' within the church, both prays with us, and acts with us where possible, for the objects of our prayer."[6]

Praising God is an important aspect of prayer, and the angels specialize in it. The liturgy abounds with references to angels. In the Mass, for example,

---

6. Origen, *On Prayer*, chap. 6. http://www.ccel.org/ccel/origen/ prayer.vii.html.

the Church prays that our sacrifice of praise may be brought before God through the ministry of angels. The Church on earth joins its praise to that of the angels, praying the "Holy, holy, holy…" in union with all the hosts of heaven.

"In her liturgy, the Church joins with the angels to adore the thrice-holy God" (*CCC*, no. 335).

In all of these ways, as the angel of peace, of repentance, and of prayer, our guardian angel helps us throughout life. And when we finally complete our earthly sojourn and prepare to meet God, our angel will be with us, to usher us into the joy of eternal life.

What Else Do We Know About the Angels?

"Just so, I tell you, there is joy
in the presence of the angels of God
over one sinner who repents."

— LUKE 15:10

Thinking About Angels

It's hard to think about the angels because we can't see them. We know by our faith that they exist because God created them. But where exactly do they fit into the whole scheme of things? If our faith didn't tell us that angels exist, we might have guessed it by thinking about the created world.

Imagine going for a walk in the woods. As you walk along a shaded trail, you're bound to see any number of rocks. The rocks exist but they aren't alive. As you continue on the trail, you'll see various types of plants: ferns, weeds, flowers, and trees. Unlike rocks, the plants are alive. They grow and require nutrients. The leaves of the plants bend toward the sun, straining to get the light they need.

Going farther into the woods, you will probably see different types of animals: birds, chipmunks, squirrels, foxes, deer, or even bears. Like plants, they are alive, but unlike plants, they can move around freely and can see, hear, eat, and bark, growl, chirp,

or make other sounds. Some even communicate
with one another in certain ways.

Neither rocks, plants, nor animals, however, can
write books, launch a rocket into space, pray, or
develop rich interpersonal relationships that can
last many years and endure despite great distances.
But people can. We can do these things because we
are rational, with minds and wills. We are also
bodily beings. So human beings are unique in the
world because we unite the material world with the
spiritual world.

As we see this progression from rocks to plants
to animals to people, we may wonder whether there
is a further step. Are there beings who are not at all
material, but purely spiritual beings? Yes! They are
the angels. While reason alone might speculate
about angels' existence without being able to prove
it, by our faith we know that they do exist.

Angels have been called "minds without bodies." They are not composed of matter. They are
spiritual substances who are intelligent and free,
having their own minds and wills. The angels are
personal beings.

In previous chapters we looked at some of the
ways angels are portrayed in the Bible, and what
Scripture teaches us about them. Through the centuries, the Catholic Church has only made a few

official statements about the angels. First, the Nicene Creed, which expresses the essential faith of the Church, says that God created "all that is, seen and unseen" (*CCC*, no. 325). The "unseen" creatures the Creed refers to are the angels. While angels always were a part of the Church's ordinary teaching, nothing more explicit was officially said about them until the year 1215, at an ecumenical council called the Fourth Lateran Council. This council affirmed that God, "from the beginning of time made at once (*simul*) out of nothing both orders of creatures, the spiritual and the corporeal, that is, the angelic and the earthly, and then (*deinde*) the human creature, who as it were shares in both orders, being composed of spirit and body" (*CCC*, no. 327). In 1870, the First Vatican Council repeated that same teaching.

It shouldn't surprise us that the Church has said very little officially on the subject of angels. As a rule, the Church only defines teachings more precisely when a controversy arises and issues need to be resolved. There hasn't been a lot of controversy about the angels that would warrant the Church stepping in to make an official statement about the subject.

However, this is where things can get quite interesting. Because there is so little official teaching, theologians have a lot of room to speculate about angels. And speculate they do! Probably no theologian speculated more about the angels than Saint Thomas Aquinas. A doctor of the Church—he is called the Angelic Doctor—and one of the Church's greatest teachers, Aquinas lived in the thirteenth century. It was an exciting time of intellectual discoveries and debate. The writings of Aristotle were arriving in Western Europe after having been mostly unknown there (except for his work on logic) and neglected for centuries. Universities were flourishing, and philosophers hotly debated how Aristotle's teachings could be reconciled with the Catholic faith. Aristotle, after all, was a pagan, so some were suspicious of his teachings. But Aquinas forged a path in taking what was good and useful in Aristotle's thought and integrating it with Christian faith.

What does philosophy have to do with the angels? Angels fascinated philosophers because they gave them a way to speculate and study about pure intellects. They could not be known directly, of course, but the medieval thinkers delighted in thinking about how their philosophical ideas might apply to pure spirits. Aquinas wrote a lot about the angels. In his masterpiece, the *Summa Theologiae*, which treats all of theology, Aquinas has a lengthy treatise about the angels. Admittedly, much of it might not seem too exciting unless you're interested in abstract questions of philosophy and how the mind works. Even Aquinas' name for the angels might puzzle us. He often called them "separated substances," in the sense of being separated from matter. Much of what Aquinas wrote is speculation, not defined doctrine. But it certainly shows that angels had an important place in medieval theology.

Aquinas wrote in the question and answer format that was popular in his day. He would pose a question, present both sides of the issue, and offer his own reply. The following are a few of the questions Aquinas asks about the angels that would probably be of interest to people today. They are by no means an exhaustive summary of his work on angels, but these highlights give us a lot to think about.

How many angels are there?

We don't know the exact number of the angels. But it is reasonable to think that God created a great multitude of angels. The Bible suggests this, for example, in a vision the prophet Daniel had of God in glory in heaven: "A thousand thousands served him, and ten thousand times ten thousand stood attending him" (Dan 7:10). Aquinas offers an intriguing reason to think that there are many angels. He said that creation reflects God's glory, and that in creating the universe, God intends its perfection. The more closely a created being images God, the more that creature reflects God's perfection and makes the universe more perfect. So, reasons Aquinas, it makes sense that God would create many angels in order to better reflect his glory and make the universe more perfect. If the material world is vast, so must be the spiritual world. For example, the more scientists study the universe, the more they understand how immense it is. They can hardly count the numbers of stars and galaxies. If God created such a huge material universe, it's reasonable to think that he also created a huge spiritual universe of angels.

What are the choirs of angels?

The "choirs" of angels have nothing to do with singing! Instead, this refers to a way of arranging groups of angels in relation to one another. People in the ancient and medieval Western world loved to arrange things in order. Aquinas was especially fond of this. He spoke of three "hierarchies" of angels, each of which has three "choirs." He didn't make this up himself, since he drew on the work of Saint Gregory the Great and also another writer, Dionysius the Areopagite. Dionysius was a Christian writer who lived in the sixth century. He wrote a book called *The Celestial Hierarchy* in which he went into great detail about the different orders of angels. This book was influential because later writers mistakenly thought that this Dionysius was the one whom Saint Paul converted in Athens (see Acts 17:34). So they thought, mistakenly, that his teaching came directly from Saint Paul. The nine choirs of angels is an arrangement based on some speculation about the angels and is not part of official Church teaching. But for the record, here they are:

First hierarchy:	Seraphim
	Cherubim
	Thrones
Second hierarchy:	Dominions
	Virtues
	Powers
Third hierarchy:	Principalities
	Archangels
	Angels

The writers in the early Church did not just dream up these names, but based them on Scripture. Here are some of the references in Scripture where we find the angels being named:

The prophet Isaiah brings out the role of the seraphim in praising God:

> Seraphs were in attendance above him; each had six wings: with two they covered their faces, and with two they covered their feet, and with two they flew. And one called to another and said:
> > "Holy, holy, holy is the Lord of hosts; the whole earth is full of his glory." (Isa 6:2–3)

The cherubim are mentioned often in the Old Testament, especially in connection with the worship of God, for example:

> The LORD is king; let the peoples tremble!
> He sits enthroned upon the cherubim;
> let the earth quake! (Ps 99:1)

The other names (thrones, dominions, virtues, powers, and principalities) are based on two texts found in Saint Paul's writings. Some of the words may be translated differently in various translations, which is why they may not match exactly.

> He is the image of the invisible God, the firstborn of all creation; for in him all things in heaven and on earth were created, things visible and invisible, whether thrones or dominions or rulers or powers—all things have been created through him and for him. (Col 1:15–16)

God put this power to work in Christ when he raised him from the dead and seated him at his right hand in the heavenly places, far above all rule and authority and power and dominion, and above every name that is named, not only in this age but also in the age to come. (Eph 1:20–21)

Angels and archangels, of course, are mentioned frequently in Scripture.

Do angels have bodies?

No, angels don't have bodies. Their very nature is to be wholly spiritual beings, without bodies or any sort of material being. What about the places in Scripture where angels are said to have appeared so that people could see them? In those cases they did not actually change into bodily beings, but somehow through God's power assumes a visible form.

Do angels know the future?

When it comes to knowing the future, we can make some distinctions. It is possible for us to know for certain some things that will happen in the future, for example, that the sun will rise tomorrow. We can know that because we have some understanding of how the physical world works. In other words, we know the causes at work that guarantee that the sun will rise tomorrow. Some other things we can know with less certainty but with a certain amount of probability. For example, a good car mechanic can estimate how long a tire will last under normal driving conditions. Or a doctor treating a cancer patient can form a good opinion about the success of a certain treatment. Angels can know these things too, because their minds are very sharp, more so than ours.

But when it comes to knowing future events themselves, or exactly how things will play out, only God knows for sure. That is because everything is eternally present to God, who knows all things. Despite their sharp minds, the angels cannot know the free future. God might choose to reveal it to them, but that is outside our experience.

Can angels know our thoughts?

Only God can know what is in our hearts and minds. So angels cannot know what we're thinking. However, just as we can often get a good idea of what another person is probably thinking by reading body language, angels can do that too. We can give ourselves away by an angry look on our face or by a smile. But only God has access to the deepest places of our hearts.

Do angels have free will?

Yes, the angels have free will. As purely spiritual creatures, they are intelligent and have both minds and wills, and so they can freely choose goodness.

Are angels loving by nature?

In answering this question, Saint Thomas Aquinas takes a more philosophical point of view. This is an intriguing question because it brings out a beautiful aspect of the angels' nature, that they are loving. Saint Thomas points out that as intellectual creatures, angels have intelligence and free will, and love follows on knowledge. In other words, a person—human or angelic—loves only what is known. An angel's intellect is sharp and penetrating, so the angels can know us quite well! And they love us all the more for it.

Has it ever happened that you got to really know a person you did not particularly care for? In so doing, in seeing things through that person's eyes, you found yourself understanding where he or she was coming from—and that made it all that much easier to respond with love. Well, the angels love us so much because they can quickly grasp more of our story than most of our friends and family members will ever come to know. They see, better than we do, the odds we're up against, the effort that we put into things that often fall apart—and through all of this they find our good qualities.

What was the sin of the angels?

Because the angels are purely spiritual beings and don't have bodies, many of the sins we commit aren't even possible for them. For example, an angel can't sin by gluttony, lust, drunkenness, or any of the many other ways we sin through our bodies. But angels could commit "spiritual" sins, that is, sins committed in their spirits, through their minds and wills: pride and envy.

We don't know exactly of what the sin of the angels consisted. Christian writers through the centuries have speculated about this. Saint Thomas thinks that the devil's sin was wanting to be like God, but in the wrong way. The devil rejected God's grace, which would have made him like God in a supernatural way. Instead, the devil wanted to find his ultimate happiness through his own power in a way that made him reject God's love. The words "I will not serve" capture that attitude. The irony of it all is that by sinning, Satan threw away what was really good for him and would have made him happy.

Did a majority of the angels sin?

We have no direct knowledge about this. But Saint Thomas Aquinas answers confidently that no, the majority of the angels did not sin. The reason he gives is an encouraging one. Ultimately, sin goes against the nature of created rational beings such as the angels. While it is certainly possible to act against nature, that's more the exception than the rule. In most cases, nature wins out. Angels are loving by nature, and so it is reasonable to think that the majority of them did not sin but remained loyal to God. Even among human beings, the majority of people are not maliciously evil. While we are sinful creatures, most of our sins are sins of weakness because we're attracted to various pleasures. Most people recoil naturally from extremely cruel acts such as murder or torture and live decent lives.

Mary and the Angels

*Today the holy Virgin Mary
is exalted above the choirs of angels
to the heavenly kingdom.*

— Ancient antiphon for the feast
of the Assumption

Queen of Angels

"Our Lady of the Angels" is a popular title for Mary. In fact, it's probably one of her most used titles, even though many people who use it don't think about its religious meaning. That's because the name of one of the biggest cities in the United States, Los Angeles, is derived from it.

The story goes back to 1769. A Franciscan priest, Father Juan Crespi, was traveling with an expedition in southern California. On August 2, they came upon a beautiful river, with sparkling clear water. The Spanish explorers often gave religious names to the places they came upon, especially if it was a feast day. August 2 was a feast especially honored by the Franciscans, the Feast of Saint Mary of the Angels. The small chapel that Saint Francis had been given in Assisi was dedicated to Our Lady under that title and was known as the Porziuncola, or "little portion." Father Crespi named the river *Nuestra Señora de los Angeles de la Porciúncula*. The area was eventually settled, and given the name *El Pueblo de Nuestra Señora la Reina de los*

Angeles de Porciúncula, or, more simply, *El Pueblo de la Reina de Los Angeles*.[7] So the name "Los Angeles" honors not only the angels in general, but also specifically Mary as Queen of the Angels.

What relationship does Mary have with the angels? Scripture and the Church's teaching are our guides, but the Church has not said very much specifically about Mary and the angels. In Scripture, however, we have the lovely annunciation account in which the Angel Gabriel visits Mary and invites her to become the Mother of God. As we have already seen, the account is found in Saint Luke's Gospel. First, Luke tells us that the angel's name is Gabriel. That's an important detail, since usually when angels are mentioned in the Gospels they are not named. For example, when Jesus was in agony in the Garden of Gethsemane, Luke tells us that an angel came to comfort him. But he doesn't tell us the name of that angel.

The annunciation account gives us two aspects about Mary's relationship with the angels. The first one shows us how the angels are connected with joy. The second one shows us how the angel Gabriel

---

7. There is still some debate about the details of the city's name; see Bob Pool, "City of Angels' First Name Still Bedevils Historians," *Los Angeles Times*, March 26, 2005.

proclaimed to Mary the Good News of the Gospel. Putting both of these aspects together, we find out that the angels bring joy by telling people about Jesus. That gives us a clue as to how we, too, can find happiness in living our Christian lives. Let's look more closely at these two things.

The Joy the Angel Brings

Gabriel's first word to Mary is *chaïré*, a Greek word meaning "rejoice." The angel invites Mary to rejoice because God has chosen her for a most special mission. But if Gabriel is telling Mary to rejoice, why is the most popular Marian prayer called the "Hail Mary" and not the "Rejoice Mary?" It's because of the way the Gospels were translated into Latin. The Latin *Vulgate Bible*, translated by Saint Jerome, uses the words "Ave Maria." In Latin, "ave" is a greeting, translated as "hail." The Latin Bible was used extensively in the Church in the West (mainly Europe), and became the basis for the prayer we know as the Hail Mary. Western writers also liked to contrast Eve (Eva in Latin) with Mary, using a play on words of changing Eva into Ave.

In the Eastern Church, however, the people could read Greek, so they had a better sense of the invitation to joy that Gabriel was extending to

Mary. Many of the Greek Fathers of the Church wrote about joy in connection with the annunciation. The famous Marian hymn of the East, called the Akathist Hymn, constantly uses the refrain "rejoice" in relation to the annunciation.

Gabriel was telling Mary to rejoice because she would be the mother of the Savior, our Lord Jesus Christ. He would save his people from their sins. Mary is sometimes called the Daughter of Zion. The Hebrew prophets often used this term in relation to Jerusalem and the people of Israel. In many passages in the Old Testament, the theme of the Daughter of Zion is related to joy. For example, the prophet Zephaniah says,

> Sing aloud, O daughter Zion;
> shout, O Israel!
> Rejoice and exult with all your heart,
> O daughter Jerusalem!
> The LORD has taken away the judgments
>   against you,
> he has turned away your enemies.
> The king of Israel, the LORD, is in your midst;
> you shall fear disaster no more.
> (Zeph 3:14–15)

God was always present with his people. But now he was coming among us in a way never before dreamed of. At the annunciation, the second Person of the Trinity took on flesh and became one of us. Mary had great reason to rejoice. And it was an angel who brought her this wonderful news.

Today we still have reason to rejoice over it. God is with us and will never abandon us. No matter what difficulties life brings, we can always turn to Jesus, who is always there to help us. And that gives us great reasons to rejoice.

The Angelus Prayer

In Catholic tradition the Angelus is a prayer that commemorates the annunciation (see page 99). This prayer developed over centuries, and is prayed three times during the day: in the morning, at noon, and in the evening. Church bells ring at these times to remind us to pray the Angelus in honor of the Incarnation of our Lord Jesus Christ. It is the Christian call to prayer.[8]

The very name "angelus," of course, is derived from the word "angel." This prayer is one concrete expression of the way that devotion to the angels has become part of our Catholic life. While praying

---

8. See "The Angelus Project" by Sister Anne Joan Flanagan for a beautiful video presentation on how to pray the Angelus: http://calltoprayer.blogspot.com.

this prayer, the themes of joy over the Incarnation and of the joy of telling others about Jesus Christ come to mind.

The Angels and the Assumption

Although we don't have an account of it in Scripture, it is a teaching of the Catholic faith that at the end of her life, Mary was assumed body and soul into heavenly glory. Pope Pius XII proclaimed this as a dogma of the faith in the year 1950. But the Church has believed in this teaching from the early centuries.

Several of the Fathers of the Church in the East wrote about the assumption and spoke of the angels in connection with it. They spoke of how the angels accompanied Mary into heaven. Saint John of Damascus in particular wrote beautifully about Mary's assumption, as in this passage:

> Today the holy Virgin of virgins is presented in the heavenly temple.... Today the sacred and living ark of the living God, who conceived her Creator himself, takes up her abode in the temple of God, not made by hands. David, her forefather, rejoices. Angels and Archangels are in jubilation, Powers exult, Principalities and

Dominions, Virtues and Thrones are in gladness: Cherubim and Seraphim magnify God. Not the least of their praise is it to refer praise to the Mother of Glory.[9]

"Queen of Angels" is a popular title for Mary, used in the Litany of Loreto and other prayers. Many works of art have depicted Mary with the angels. With the angels, we honor her as our loving Mother and turn to her with confidence in all our needs.

9. Saint John Damascene, *Homily 2 on the Assumption*, http://www. ccel.org/ccel/damascus/icons.i.viii.html.

Walking with the Angels

*The angel of the LORD encamps
around those who fear him,
and delivers them.*

— PSALM 34:7

Do angels ever manifest themselves to us? They certainly have, and at times they come to our aid in more visible ways. The following stories are true accounts from people who believe they were helped by an angel who intervened in a special way. While such stories are not matters of faith, they can remind us of the endless variety of ways that God sends angels to help us. Sometimes he might send an angel directly, and at other times he might work through people who are "angels among us." They come into our lives in mysterious ways, as Scripture reminds us: "Do not neglect to show hospitality to strangers, for by doing that some have entertained angels without knowing it" (Heb 13:2).

Laura N., Minnesota

A few weeks before my fifth child was born I began to pray to my guardian angel that I would have no pain during the delivery. My previous baby was over ten pounds, and it had been a very difficult delivery. When I went into labor again, I was afraid, the whole time I was lying there, trying to be brave for my family. A war was going on inside my head. I had been playing with the idea of praying out loud (which I never do, unless it's prescribed prayer and/or with a group of people) if things got too intense. I was a bundle of nerves and couldn't relax, even though I didn't have any pain. Right before I started to feel an urge to push, I panicked and started to cry. The doctor was alarmed and asked if I was in any pain. I couldn't describe how I was feeling, but my sister knew. She told the doctor that I didn't *exactly* feel pain but that I was so afraid of pain that every little bit of pressure or *hint* of pain was making me worried about the future pain! The doctor looked relieved. I started to feel the pressure of the baby coming (for the first time with any of the children … because I had *no pain*! I have had epidurals before, and they would work temporarily but they never lasted … this one did!) and thought it might be a good time to try my experiment.

I took a deep breath and said, "Okay, guardian angel, now might be a good time to help!" I started pushing. In between the first and second push, I was joking and laughing because I knew everything would be okay. I just had a wave of peace come over me that I've never felt before. I said, "Okay, guardian angel, be with me now and make this the last push!" And right then Mariela was born.

I don't know if it's because of my guardian angel, or because of the hundreds of prayers that were going up to the Lord at that very moment, but either way, this is how it happened. I'll always be grateful for the *one* chance to have a baby with no pain.

Veronica H., Ontario, Canada

The summer after my baptism into the Catholic faith as an adult convert, my grandmother was diagnosed with cancer. She had a grim prognosis. She was a tough woman who had lived a very hard life, but she was full of love for those she cared about. She had never been baptized, and I don't think that she ever seriously thought about Christianity. She had some interest in New Age and the occult. I didn't want her to leave this world without ever knowing Christ.

I was away at school when she first became ill, and it was impossible for me to be with her in person for most of her last days. So, every day for months, I went to Mass, begging for her to come to Christ, and every night I prayed the Divine Mercy Chaplet for her. By early fall, my grandmother had moved in with my mother. One afternoon, my grandmother was alone in her room, and she started screaming for my mother, insisting that she had seen an angel in her room, holding his hand out to her. When my mother ran in, he disappeared.

I admit I am skeptical. At the time, grandmother wasn't on drugs strong enough to cause hallucinations, and the tumors had not yet spread to her brain. However, a number of other possible explanations could account for the incident. I don't know what really happened in that room, but it doesn't matter. What matters more is this: My grandmother almost immediately began asking to be baptized, and on the Feast of Christ the King, she received the sacraments of Baptism, Confirmation, the Eucharist, and Anointing of the Sick.

When I came to visit her for the Christmas holidays, she was extremely ill but still so loving and joyful. She wanted a rosary and asked me how to pray it, so I gave her mine and taught her how to use it. Later, I found out that most nights she fell asleep clutching it, as she called out to the Blessed Virgin whenever the suffering was too much for her. Eventually, grandmother was buried with it.

My grandmother suffered much in those last days, but to the end she did it with strength, grace, and humility. She died at dawn on January 7, the day some Eastern Churches celebrate Christmas. I am so grateful for the gift the Lord gave my grandmother, my family, and myself when he answered my most fervent prayers and brought my grandmother home. His mercy has no limit.

SISTER KATHRYN H., MASSACHUSETTS

It was a perfect autumn day. I was home on vacation and was walking back to my parents' house after Mass. The street had no sidewalk and was quite treacherous with its uneven pavement and narrow lanes. I tripped on a hole disguised by fallen leaves and went sprawling into the road, landing on my right arm. I panicked, seeing the oncoming traffic, and I tried to get up, but my right arm hung uselessly at my side. I could see cars coming over the hill about 500 feet away from me. Raising my left hand to attract attention, I kept repeating, "Please don't run me over." I spied my glasses just within reach and I somehow managed to grab them and roll off the road before the traffic reached me. I knelt about six inches away from the passing cars. One after the other, they sped by. No one stopped.

"How am I going to get up?" I desperately thought while the world around me got strangely quiet. I tried to stand during a lull in the traffic and fell back into a sitting position. A call to my dad's cell phone only allowed me to leave a message. Then I called my parents' home. No answer. I wondered how my parents would ever find me, and I tried to lean away from the traffic. I have never felt so scared and alone. I thought about the parable of the Good Samaritan and what the victim must have felt when he was left for dead. I realized that I, too, have passed people by who had been lying "on the side of the roads" of my daily life. It was a lesson I vowed never to forget.

Suddenly, an older man dressed in gray appeared in front of me. I didn't see where he had come from. "Sister, do you need help?" he asked. I told him I couldn't get up and that I needed help to get to my father's house down the next road. He took my left hand, told me to brace myself on his foot and pulled me straight up. "Thank you. Please take me home." He went to call the police to get me to an emergency room. While I stood there trying to keep my balance, a woman came out of a house and walked me home. We never heard police sirens and never saw the man again. Was he an angel or a kind old man? I don't know, but I do know he was exceptionally strong. In the following days others attempted to pull me up from low sofas by grasping my good hand. In every case it took several attempts to get me on my feet. But the man in gray had pulled me up effortlessly on the first try. He had done exactly what was needed and had disappeared. Suddenly I remembered other stories from sisters in my community who had been helped by a mysterious man in gray, whom we always thought was an angel. Whether it was he or not that day, I will always believe in angels.

Sister Maureen M., Ontario, Canada

My mother, Catherine, had a great devotion to Saint Michael the Archangel, the patron of her home parish in Flushing, New York. She had graduated from the parish school and was married in her parish church. Her devotion to the Archangel Michael led her to beg his intercession to find a way to ensure that her two daughters could attend the nearest parochial school.

My parents soon moved out to Long Island, settling in an established parish that had a sizable church, rectory, convent, and elementary school. But during those baby boom years, more parishes were needed to accommodate the growing population. So our parish was divided. Suddenly our home was in the boundaries of a new parish consisting only of a piece of property! It had no church—and worse yet—no school! But we continued to attend

Sunday Mass at the established parish, and my mother began her prayer vigil to get us into the school.

One day during the announcements after Mass, a request was made for any ladies who might wish to help care for the altar linens. My mother thought, "I know how to do that," but promptly dismissed the thought from her mind. After Mass, on the way to the car, deep in her own thoughts, my mother heard a voice call her, "Mrs. M., aren't you going to see the sacristan about the altar linens?" Startled, she looked up and saw a tall young man in front of her. She later told me, "He had on a suit of the most beautiful material I've ever seen, almost iridescent." She did not get a good look at his face because she was "so taken" by the material of his beautiful suit.

"Oh, of course," she replied.

"The sacristan is coming now. Go ahead," the young man prompted.

A bit dazed, she murmured, "Thank you," and headed over to sign up. When she turned around, he was gone.

My mother told me that she had searched for him at church for a long time but never saw him again. She was convinced that Saint Michael answered her prayer. She remembered distinctly *that he had called her by name*, which she had thought odd since we had only been living there for a short time and did not yet know many people.

My mother joined the Ladies Altar Society, and I was among the last of the first graders admitted to the parish school from outside the parish boundaries. My mother is convinced that God sent Saint Michael to answer her prayer. In gratitude, my mother continued to care for the altar linens many years after I graduated from high school.

SISTER SHARON ANNE L., MASSACHUSETTS

All through my life I have been very devoted to my guardian angel, and I often pray to the angels for protection and help. On two occasions I experienced this in a particular way. The first occurred several years ago when I was visiting some homes in an apartment building with another sister. We were going door to door with our religious books and magazines, inviting people to read the word of God in various forms. We had finished knocking on all the doors of the first two floors of the building. However, no one had answered and no one seemed to be around. We then made our way to the third floor and had walked halfway up the stairway. Suddenly a woman opened her door, came out onto the landing, and called out, "Who are you?" We explained who we were, and she said, "I'm not interested." Just then her dog ran out of the apartment. When he saw us, he growled, bared his teeth, and jumped off the landing to attack us. When I saw the dog coming, I immediately shouted, "Angel of God!" Suddenly, the dog was swung around in midair as if someone had slapped its side. It landed on the stairs, away from us, and meekly turned around and ran whimpering up the stairs. I believe that my guardian angel protected us from danger that day.

Another incident occurred when I was assigned to working with the young women who entered our community wishing to become sisters. One night I had retired for the evening and prayed to my guardian angel as I always did. After I had fallen asleep, one of the young women knocked on my door. She said, "What is it, Sister? You called me." But I hadn't called her. As she turned to go back to her room, she suddenly saw smoke coming from the end of our building complex. "Look, there's smoke!" she called out. I went to the window and saw a fire at the far end of the building. I woke up the other sisters on the floor and called the fire department. When the fire truck arrived, the firefighters found that a burning car had been deliberately parked near the side of the building. They quickly extinguished the fire. One of them told me that we had called them just in time, because the car had been burning near a window that was on the verge of bursting under the pressure from the heat of the flames. If that had happened, the fire would have quickly spread into the basement of that building, which was where we stored all the paper we used for the printing presses (in those days we did our own printing for our publishing house). If the paper had caught fire it would have been almost impossible to put out. I believe that our guardian angels alerted us to the danger that night.

ANGELA P., LOUISIANA

Nothing seemed to work. No matter how hard I tried, I just couldn't be happy. An awful weight was hanging on me: guilt and depression added to the trauma of rape. Even after I made a Cursillo retreat and forgave the rapist in my heart, the guilt and the low self-esteem that goes with it returned because I had only made a first step, forgiveness. I still thought of myself as unredeemable, ruined. It clouded every friendship and activity that touched my life.

No one seemed to approve of or want me. I had no education, friends were moving on. I had no job, so all I did was sit and think. I felt worthless, and my life seemed hopeless. One day, I couldn't stand the pain anymore. The thought that I would be better off dead had tormented me daily. In my bathroom mirror, I looked at myself. I did not even know who I was. Frightened by what I was now facing, all I could think of was that I could not do it anymore. I could not go on living like this, with no hope and no life.

Suddenly I remembered that my dad had a straight razor in the cabinet. I found it. Slowly I took it out of the blue paper sleeve and put it on the counter. My fear of blood made me hesitate. I don't like pain either, but which pain was worse? I didn't know anymore. I could only think that the pain would never end. Crying and looking at that person in the mirror staring back at me, I began to sob in despair. Just then a voice came into my heart from behind me, to the right. I felt the presence before it spoke, and I expected it to mock me. But I felt no danger or hatred, so I thought maybe it was a friend, not a foe. I sensed it was my guardian angel. I believe that it was. I could hear the voice speak inside me saying, "So that's it. You're just going to let him win? So he's won! Just like that?!

It's all over, then. That's what he wants, you know, and you're just going to give it to him? Just like that! Then he's won." At first I thought the angel meant the rapist, but then I realized he meant Satan. I suddenly grew indignant and thought "Oh, no, he's not! Nobody is winning anything here!" I got angry enough to fight back. That is how my angel used reason to tick me off until God could reach me. I left home and went to a new town, where I met the man who is now my husband.

BERNADETTE R., CALIFORNIA

When I was about ten or eleven years old, my mother and I were in our station wagon driving along a street that did not have much traffic. We stopped at a red light, but my mother did not start to accelerate when the light turned green. Whenever that happened, I used to gently tell my mother that the light had turned green. But that time, for some reason, my mother remained immobile. A few seconds later, a car flew through the red light. My mom and I sat there stunned, realizing that I would probably have been killed if she had started to accelerate when the light turned green. As soon as she could catch her breath to speak, my mother turned to me and said, "Something told me not move. It must have been my guardian angel because every time I get in the car to drive, I always say a prayer to my guardian angel." I owe my life to whoever that angel is!

LYNN G., NEW YORK

When Pope John Paul II came to New York in 1995, I was part of the choir for the Mass in Central Park. My friend, Carmelina, had white tickets to go to the event with her sister-in-law, Irene. The tickets were organized by color, and I explained to Carmelina what the codes meant. Red was for invited guests who sat right in front of the huge altar. Green was located behind the red section, no chairs but an unblocked view of the altar. The blue areas were on the sides, and the white tickets just got you into the park so you could be there.

The Mass was glorious! Escaping his handlers, Pope John Paul II went over to our group, cheered, and clapped his hands; he walked down to the two cantors at the front of the massive stage/altar to kiss and thank them for their beautiful cantoring. The entire experience remains the single greatest event in my twenty years of singing for the Lord.

The next day my sister, Judy, called to tell me Carmelina would be calling to thank me for the tickets. I explained that I hadn't given her tickets but had only told her about the ticket color system. "You didn't give Carmelina and Irene six green tickets before the Mass yesterday?" No, I hadn't. How could she even think I could find someone with 450,000 people in the park, not to mention that I was sequestered in the holding pen backstage. What on earth were they talking about?!

Carmelina and Irene said they got into the park with their white tickets and it was crowded beyond their expectations. They couldn't even see a Jumbotron. They were actually planning on leaving and going back to Irene's apartment to watch the Mass on TV. One woman in a wheelchair was crying because she and her three friends had driven all the way from Pennsylvania to see the Pope and now they couldn't even see or hear anything. As they were speaking with the woman in the wheelchair, so the story goes, I came "running up to them" through the crowd and said to Carmelina and Irene, "I'm so glad I found you! I have these green tickets for you. Go that way and you'll be able to see the Pope." I gave them six tickets and hurried off, they assumed, to go back to the choir. They invited the crying woman in the wheelchair and her friends to come with them. They were able to get all the way up to a temporary fence directly behind the seated guests, and could see the Pope with their own eyes and hear the entire Mass.

Carmelina couldn't wait to thank me for the tickets and tell me how much it meant to the woman in the wheelchair. I couldn't convince either her or Irene that it wasn't I who came running up to them. There was no physical way I could have been there. Impossible. But, something we know for sure is that nothing is impossible with God.

Could it really have been an angel? Or was someone nearby hearing their conversation, had six tickets she decided not to use, and just offered them those tickets? Maybe. Except that both Carmelina and Irene insisted absolutely that it was me, wearing jeans, a white shirt, and black blazer, which was what I had on when I saw them the day before the Mass.

The woman in the wheelchair was so desperate to see the Pope, believing she would get well if she could only see him with her own eyes. Could God have sent the angel to show her the way, using Carmelina, Irene, and me as the vessels, thus extending John Paul II's powerful spirit to her? How I wish we could find her now.

We are called to expect, acknowledge, and proclaim these wonderful glimpses of heaven by which the Lord blesses us. Something supernatural and grace-filled happened that day in Central Park. Somebody's angel stepped into time and showed us a miracle, which I believe was from the holiness of John Paul II. We are all the better for it, especially the woman in the wheelchair whose prayer to see him with her own eyes was answered.

Patricia M., Pennsylvania

I've named my guardian angel Timothy. I know he is always present (and I somehow get the feeling of a "he," hence Timothy), and he has helped and protected me in many ways and situations. However, I sense that Timothy has two areas that are his "specialties." The first one is that he always gets me up on time so that I never oversleep, even when I have been very tired. Once I was in a very deep sleep and I heard someone calling my name. Then I felt my bed rocking, as if someone was leaning on it and pushing it up and down. As I gradually awoke, I was wondering why I hadn't heard anyone come in. The bedroom door was heavy, and the latch always clicked loudly when opened or closed. When I opened my eyes I expected to see someone standing at the foot of my bed; however, the room was empty.

Timothy's second specialty concerns any electronic equipment, such as printers and computers. If something isn't working or one machine isn't "talking" to another, I simply say a couple "Angel of God" prayers and it works. Here are two examples: I recently had problems with our main printer at work, so that it would only print on a certain stock of paper. I was working late and needed to print a letter on letterhead, which was not the correct stock for this printer. I forgot and put the letterhead in, and the printer churned out a crumpled mess. No other printer was available and I needed to get this letter out. I said an "Angel of God," tried again, and a perfect letter came out. I was amazed at Timothy's expertise because this printer would never take any other paper.

A new area of electronics for Timothy is wireless networking. Once I was trying to connect to a system and had all the correct numbers, but the system just would not connect, even after two hours of effort. Then I remembered Timothy. I started to pray and turned around to pick up a piece of paper. When I turned back, I was online. I thank God for my "electronically savvy" and very vigilant guardian angel.

Devotions and Prayers

And the smoke of the incense,
with the prayers of the saints,
rose before God from the hand of the angel.

— REVELATION 8:4

The Angelus

The angel of the Lord declared unto Mary.
And she conceived of the Holy Spirit.

Hail Mary, full of grace, the Lord is with you,
blessed are you among women,
and blessed is the fruit of your womb, Jesus.
Holy Mary, Mother of God, pray for us sinners,
now and at the hour of our death. Amen.

Behold the handmaid of the Lord,
be it done unto me according to your word.
Hail Mary....

And the Word was made flesh.
And dwelt among us.
Hail Mary....

Pray for us, O Holy Mother of God, that we may be made worthy of the promises of Christ.

Let us pray:

Pour forth, we beseech you, O Lord, your grace into our hearts, that we, to whom the Incarnation of Christ, your Son, was made known by the message of an angel, may by his passion and cross be brought to the glory of his resurrection, through the same Christ our Lord. Amen.

The Guardian Angel Prayer

Angel of God, my guardian dear, to whom God's love entrusts me here, ever this day be at my side, to light and guard, to rule and guide. Amen.

Prayer to the Guardian Angel
for Guidance in Life

My guardian angel, I thank the Lord for having sent you to guide me through the ways of life. Help me to pay attention to the gentle ways that you use to lead me closer to God each day. When I am facing an important decision, help me to choose the course of action that will most please the Lord. When I am facing any difficulty, help me to keep on going when I want to quit. Strengthen my relationships with family and friends, so that together we may find happiness in life and eternal joy in the life to come. Amen.

--------❦❧--------

Prayer for One's Family

*H*eavenly Father, I thank you for the gift of my family and for the many joys and blessings that have come to me through each of them. Help me to appreciate the uniqueness of each person while rejoicing in our common family bonds. Through the intercession of our guardian angels, I ask you to protect my family from the evils of this world. Grant us all the power to forgive when we have been hurt and the humility to ask for forgiveness when we have caused pain. Unite us in the love of your Son, Jesus, that we may be a sign of the unity you desire for all humanity.

Holy angels, intercede for us. Amen.

--------❦❧--------

Prayer of Thanksgiving for the Guardian Angel

*H*eavenly Father, I thank your infinite goodness for having entrusted me to the care of an angel. I also thank you, my guardian angel, for accompanying me daily on my return journey to my heavenly Father. Your holy inspirations, your continual protection against spiritual and physical dangers, and your powerful prayers to God give me great comfort and sure hope.

Blessed James Alberione

Prayer for Our Nation
in a Time of Great Need

*H*oly angels, you whom God has sent to watch over and guard our nation, we ask for your help and intercession during this time of great national need. Inspire our civic leaders with wisdom so they may choose the right paths. Protect all the people of this country, especially the children, from every danger to spirit and body. May we seek to serve one another's needs and so build a society that will lead to the civilization of truth and love, where God will reign over all. Amen.

Prayer to the Angel Who Came to Jesus in the Garden of Gethsemane

O holy angel, who came to strengthen Jesus Christ our Lord, come and strengthen me also; come and do not delay!

Saint Pius X

--------❦◌❧--------

The Guardian Angel

My oldest friend, mine from the hour
When first I drew my breath;
My faithful friend, that shall be mine,
Unfailing, till my death;
Thou hast been ever at my side;
My Maker to thy trust
Consign'd my soul, what time He framed
The infant child of dust.
No beating heart in holy prayer,
No faith, inform'd aright,
Gave me to Joseph's tutelage,
Or Michael's conquering might.
Nor patron Saint, nor Mary's love,
The dearest and the best,

Has known my being as thou hast known,
And blest, as thou hast blest.
Thou wast my sponsor at the font;
And thou, each budding year,
Didst whisper elements of truth
Into my childish ear.
And when, ere boyhood yet was gone,
My rebel spirit fell,
Ah! thou didst see, and shudder too,
Yet bear each deed of Hell.
And then in turn, when judgments came,
And scared me back again,
Thy quick soft breath was near to soothe
And hallow every pain.
Oh! who of all thy toils and cares
Can tell the tale complete,
To place me under Mary's smile,
And Peter's royal feet!
And thou wilt hang about my bed,
When life is ebbing low;
Of doubt, impatience, and of gloom,
The jealous, sleepless foe.
Mine, when I stand before the Judge;
And mine, if spared to stay
Within the golden furnace, till

My sin is burn'd away.
And mine, O Brother of my soul,
When my release shall come;
Thy gentle arms shall lift me then,
Thy wings shall waft me home.

John Henry Cardinal Newman

PRAYERS TO SAINT MICHAEL

Novena to Saint Michael and the Angels

Saint Michael, reflection of God's beauty, holiness, and majesty,

— *intercede for us before God's holy throne.*

You are the chosen protector of all God's people,

— *present my prayer of praise and supplication at the throne of God.*

First Day

Saint Michael, reflection of God's beauty…

O God, through the intercession of Saint Michael and the heavenly choir of the Seraphim, instill in my heart the flame of charity, that I may love you with my whole heart and seek to love others as you love me. Keep me faithful to your love today, and open my heart to receive the blessings you want to pour out on me, especially the grace I ask for at this time.

(Mention your petition and pray one Our Father, Hail Mary, and Glory.)

Second Day

Saint Michael, reflection of God's beauty...

O God, through the intercession of Saint Michael and the heavenly choir of the Cherubim, grant that I may leave aside all that may lead me to sin and follow only the path of Christian holiness. Keep me faithful to your love today, and open my heart to receive the blessings you want to pour out on me, especially the grace I ask for at this time.

(Mention your petition and pray one Our Father, Hail Mary, and Glory.)

Third Day

Saint Michael, reflection of God's beauty...

O God, through the intercession of Saint Michael and the heavenly choir of the thrones, fill my heart with a sincere spirit of gentleness and humility. Keep me faithful to your love today, and open my heart to receive the blessings you want to pour out on me, especially the grace I ask for at this time.

(Mention your petition and pray one Our Father, Hail Mary, and Glory.)

FOURTH DAY

Saint Michael, reflection of God's beauty...

O God, through the intercession of Saint Michael and the heavenly choir of the Dominions, grant that I may ever keep control over my senses so that my thoughts, words, and actions may always serve your kingdom here on earth. Keep me faithful to your love today, and open my heart to receive the blessings you want to pour out on me, especially the grace I ask for at this time.

(Mention your petition and pray one Our Father, Hail Mary, and Glory.)

FIFTH DAY

Saint Michael, reflection of God's beauty...

O God, through the intercession of Saint Michael and the heavenly choir of the Powers, keep temptation far from me and defend me against the deceits of the Evil One. Keep me faithful to your love today, and open my heart to receive the blessings you want to pour out on me, especially the grace I ask for at this time.

(Mention your petition and pray one Our Father, Hail Mary, and Glory.)

Sixth Day

Saint Michael, reflection of God's beauty...

O God, through the intercession of Saint Michael and the heavenly choir of the Virtues, lead me along the path to holiness of life that I may love and serve others in your name. Keep me faithful to your love today, and open my heart to receive the blessings you want to pour out on me, especially the grace I ask for at this time.

(Mention your petition and pray one Our Father, Hail Mary, and Glory.)

Seventh Day

Saint Michael, reflection of God's beauty...

O God, through the intercession of Saint Michael and the heavenly choir of the Principalities, fill my heart with a spirit of true and sincere obedience and increase my desire to do your will in all things. Keep me faithful to your love today, and open my heart to receive the blessings you want to pour out on me, especially the grace I ask for at this time.

(Mention your petition and pray one Our Father, Hail Mary, and Glory.)

EIGHTH DAY

Saint Michael, reflection of God's beauty. . .

O God, through the intercession of Saint Michael and the heavenly choir of the Archangels, increase my faith and grant me perseverance in doing good works that I may enjoy everlasting life in your presence. Keep me faithful to your love today, and open my heart to receive the blessings you want to pour out on me, especially the grace I ask for at this time.

(Mention your petition and pray one Our Father, Hail Mary, and Glory.)

NINTH DAY

Saint Michael, reflection of God's beauty. . .

O God, through the intercession of Saint Michael and the heavenly choir of the Angels, keep me and my loved ones from sin and evil here on earth, and after death lead us into the everlasting joy of heaven. Keep me faithful to your love today, and open my heart to receive the blessings you want to pour out on me, especially the grace I ask for at this time.

(Mention your petition and pray one Our Father, Hail Mary, and Glory.)

To Saint Michael, Protector of God's People

Saint Michael the Archangel, defend us in the battle. Be our defense against the wickedness and deceit of the devil. May God rebuke him, we humbly pray. And you, O prince of the heavenly host, by the power of God banish into hell Satan and the other evil spirits who roam through the world seeking the ruin of souls. Amen.

Prayer in Time of Difficulty

Glorious Saint Michael, prince of the heavenly hosts, valiant defender of the Church, you are always ready to assist the People of God in time of adversity. Be with me now in my hour of difficulty, that I may walk steadfastly along the way of discipleship. I have confidence that through your intercession the Lord will grant me all the spiritual grace and strength I need to follow Jesus more closely, and that one day I may rejoice forever with you in heaven. Amen.

Prayer for Perseverance

O God, you made blessed Michael, your archangel, victorious in the battle against evil. We ask that, fortified by the cross of your Son, we too may be victorious in the spiritual conflicts we face in our daily lives. Through the intercession of Saint Michael, deliver us from all evil and keep temptation far from us. Guide us to faithfully follow your will and to walk in the way of your commandments. We ask this through Christ, our Lord. Amen.

Prayer for the Church

Glorious Saint Michael, guardian and defender of the Church of Jesus Christ, come to the assistance of the Church in this time of need. Guard the Pope with special care, and intercede for him that he may carry out his ministry in peace and joy. Obtain for bishops the spiritual gifts necessary to be true shepherds of the flocks given to their care. Ask God to give our priests the courage they need to meet the challenges of their vocation. For men and women religious, ask that they be granted enthusiasm for their calling and a loving reverence for all those whom they serve in their varied ministries. For the laity in the Church, ask for the gift of fidelity to Christ and to their call to discipleship. For those who have distanced themselves from the Church, inspire them to undertake the interior journey that will lead them back to the grace of the sacraments. For all Christians, ask for the gift of unity, and ask the Holy Spirit to inspire the hearts of all people to continue the saving work of Christ until the end of time, when we will all be united in heaven. Amen.

Prayer for Police Officers

Saint Michael, defender against the forces of evil, protect our police officers and sustain them in their never-ending struggle to defeat criminal forces in our society. Ask the Lord to keep them safe and to give them courage in the face of danger, right judgment in the face of confusion, and clarity in the face of ambiguity. Inspire them to safeguard human dignity, and keep their hearts free from anger and bitterness when confronted with so much wrong-doing.

Encourage them to be compassionate with those who are hurting, and give them self-control when confronting perpetrators. Be their constant companion and keep them safe from temptation and harm. Teach them how to live by faith in Jesus' promise that he is with us always. Teach them how to live in hope, relying on the Lord's saving power to bring them through hard times. Teach them how to live in Jesus' love that they may be light in the darkness for others.

Trusting in your powerful intercession before the throne of God, I ask that you guide all law enforcement officers along life's journey until the day they join you and all the angels in heaven to praise God for all eternity. Amen.

Prayer for a Holy Death

Saint Michael, light and confidence of souls at the hour of death, I ask you to intercede for all the dying, and invoke your assistance in the hour of my own death. Deliver me from sudden death; obtain for me the grace to live as a faithful disciple of Jesus, to detach my heart from everything worldly, and daily to gather treasures for the moment of my death. Obtain for me the grace to receive the Sacrament of the Sick well, and at the moment of my death fill my heart with sentiments of faith, hope, love, and sorrow for sins, so that I may breathe forth my soul in peace. Amen.

Adapted from the writings of Blessed James Alberione

Prayer of Praise and Thanksgiving

All-loving God, I praise, glorify, and bless you for all the graces and privileges you have bestowed upon your messenger and servant, Saint Michael. By the merits of your angels grant me your grace, and through the intercession of your Archangel Michael help me in all my needs. At the hour of my death be with me until that time when I can join the angels and saints in heaven to praise you for ever and ever. Amen.

PRAYERS IN HONOR OF SAINT GABRIEL

Prayer for an Expectant Mother

Almighty and loving God, through the power of the Holy Spirit you prepared the Virgin Mary to be the worthy mother of your own Son, Jesus. Listen to my prayer through the intercession of Saint Gabriel, your faithful servant, and protect (*name*) during her pregnancy and birthing.

Creator of Life, grant (*name*) the joy of anticipating new life within her womb, and in time of pain or distress allow her to experience your consoling presence. Grant her, Lord, the spiritual and emotional care she needs to bring her child into the world. Give (*name*) the wisdom to know how to safeguard her physical welfare so that the child she carries within her may be healthy in mind and body. May all of her children bring her joy and reflect your love for her until they may, one day, enjoy the eternal happiness of heaven. Amen.

Prayer for the Messengers of the Gospel

Saint Gabriel, you brought the good news of salvation to Mary; assist, inspire, and comfort the ministers of the Word.

Saint Gabriel, you acted as the messenger of God; intervene with your protection that the light of the Gospel may reach all peoples.

Saint Gabriel, you were the herald of Jesus, the Way, the Truth, and the Life; intercede for us, so that heaven may be filled with those who sing the hymn of glory to the Most Holy Trinity. Amen.

Based on a prayer by Blessed James Alberione

Prayer to Find Peace and Joy

Saint Gabriel, when you brought the good news to Mary about the birth of Jesus, you greeted her with the word, "Rejoice!" God was going to do something marvelous in her life, and he chose you to play an important role in that wonderful event. You are the angel of good tidings, the one who brings news of happiness and joy. I ask you to intercede for me that I may experience the peace and joy that God desires for me. When I feel discouraged or worried, help me to have great trust and confidence in the Lord, knowing that "all things work together for good for those who love God" (Rom 8:28). Pray for me that I may always have great trust in the Lord and walk under his loving care. Amen.

Prayer in Honor of Saint Gabriel

*H*eavenly Father, I thank you for having chosen Saint Gabriel from among the angels to bring to Mary the good news of the Incarnation. Mary responded to your invitation with faith and joy, and became the Mother of God. She presented to the world the Eternal Word, our Lord and Savior, Jesus Christ. But many people have still not heard the message of salvation that Jesus gave us in the Gospel.

Saint Gabriel, patron of the modern means of communication, beg Jesus, our Divine Master and Shepherd, that the Church may use these powerful means to bring the Gospel to everyone. May these gifts of God serve to uplift all people and bring them to a knowledge of truth. May they always be used in a way that builds up the dignity of human persons. Saint Gabriel, pray for us and for all those who use the modern means of communication. Amen.

PRAYERS TO SAINT RAPHAEL

Novena to Saint Raphael

This prayer can be used as a novena by praying it for nine consecutive days.

O Saint Raphael, bearer of holy joy and messenger of peace,

—— *intercede for us before God's holy throne.*

You are one of the seven angels who enter and serve before the glory of the Lord,

—— *present my prayer of praise and supplication at the throne of God.*

O God, you brought joy of spirit and health in mind and body into the lives of Tobit, Sarah, and Tobias through your holy angel, Raphael. Grant, we beseech you, the grace we ask through the intercession of Saint Raphael. Amen.

(Mention your petition and pray one Our Father, Hail Mary, and Glory.)

Prayer for Travelers

Saint Raphael, Archangel, as you protected young Tobias on his journey to a distant land, protect all those who travel today, especially (*name*). Safeguard all fathers and mothers whose work requires them to travel; protect all children who travel to and from school, to be with a parent, or to visit a relative. Watch over those who journey to preach the Gospel. Guide those responsible for operating transport vehicles, and inspire the owners of transportation systems to provide dependable and affordable means of transit. Encourage those who maintain these systems to be trustworthy in providing safe and reliable means so that all who travel will reach their destinations in comfort and safety. Amen.

A Commuter's Prayer

Saint Raphael, Archangel, you brought healing, joy, and harmony to all those you met while you journeyed with young Tobias. I, too, place myself under your protection as I commute today. Teach me how to be a bearer of God's healing peace as you were; let my words and actions reflect the kindness and compassion of Jesus. Be with me today and every day as I travel along the road of life. Amen.

A Driver's Prayer

*H*eavenly Father, grant me a steady hand and a watchful eye that I may safely reach my destination. Grant me self-control, courtesy, and freedom from aggressive behavior. Protect those who travel with me today. For those whom I drive or meet, let me be thoughtful and courteous so I can, in some small way, mirror the love Jesus has for each of us. Open the eyes of my heart that I may see beyond the road and buildings to recognize the beauty that reflects the wonders of your creation.

Saint Raphael, Archangel, be my guide and protector today. Kindly precede me and guard me. Amen.

Prayer Before Leaving for a Trip

*H*eavenly Father, we thank you for having created a great and wonderful world through which we can travel. We ask you to bless us as we are about to leave on our trip. In days past you sent your Archangel Raphael to accompany Tobias on his journey; send him now to be with us as our guide and companion.

Deliver us from all harm and keep us safe in your love. Grant that we may rejoice in all that we see and all whom we meet. Free us from restlessness and disappointment due to delays or unpleasant weather. Give us patience to accept these with a spiritual vision, seeing in these events the mystery of your loving plan.

Let us awake each day to the beauty of creation that surrounds us and to a confident awareness of your sacred presence within. May your blessing be upon us to bring us home again in safety and in peace. Amen.

Prayer for Healing

Almighty and eternal God, healer of those who trust in you, through the intercession of Saint Raphael, Archangel, hear my prayer for (*name*). In your tender mercy, restore her/him to spiritual and/or bodily health that she/he may give you thanks, praise your name, and proclaim your wondrous love to all. I ask this through Christ your Son, our Lord. Amen.

Prayer for the Choice of a Spouse

Saint Raphael, Archangel, sent by God to counsel young Tobias in the choice of a good and virtuous spouse, guide me also in this important life choice. With your help I want to meet the one who is "right for me" as a husband/wife. Through your inspiration I want my heart's choice to be the spouse the Lord would also choose for me, so that our life together will be one of mutual happiness and love. Amen.

Prayer of Praise and Thanksgiving

All-loving God, I praise, glorify, and bless you for all the graces and privileges you have bestowed upon your messenger and servant, Saint Raphael. By the merits of your angels grant me your grace, and through the intercession of your Archangel Raphael help me in all my needs. At the hour of my death be with me until that time when I can join the angels and saints in heaven to praise you forever and ever. Amen.

Afterword

Holy angels,
    mighty in spirit, who do God's bidding
    sent to guide us along the way of life
    hidden yet always present
    you help us bear the burdens we carry
       each day.

Holy angels,
    we know you only by faith.
    Protect us from evil.
    Open our ears to hear the word of God.
    Teach us wisdom.

Holy angels,
    We invite you into our lives
    so that we may always know
    that wherever we go, whatever happens,
    we are surrounded by your holy presence.

Additional Resources

Read More About the Angels

Adler, Mortimer. *The Angels and Us*. New York: Macmillan, 1982.

Aquilina, Mike. *Angels of God*. Cincinnati: Servant Books, 2009.

Aquinas, Thomas. *Summa Theologiae*. Translated by Kenelm Foster, OP. Vol. 9: *Angels*. Cambridge, UK: Blackfriars, 1968.

Brown, R. E., et al. *Mary in the New Testament*. Philadelphia: Fortress Press, 1978.

Bussagli, Marco. *Angels*. New York: Harry N. Abrams, 2007.

Daniélou, Jean. *The Angels and Their Mission According to the Fathers of the Church*. Westminster, MD: Newman Press, 1957.

de la Potterie, Ignace. *Mary in the Mystery of the Covenant*. New York: Alba House, 1992.

Giudici, Maria Pia. *The Angels: Spiritual and Exegetical Notes*. New York: Alba House, 1993.

Huber, Georges. *My Angel Will Go Before You*. Dublin: Four Courts Press, 1983.

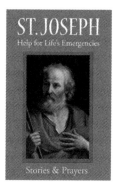

ST. JOSEPH
Help for Life's Emergencies
Compiled and Edited by
Kathryn J. Hermes, FSP

Saint Joseph, foster father of Jesus and husband of Mary, is often called on to intercede in the selling of a house. However, those with a devotion to Saint Joseph know that he can help with much more: employment, family issues, happy death, finances, divine providence, home improvement, and good health. Let the stories and prayers in this book help you open your heart to the care that Saint Joseph can provide.

Paperback   128pp.
#71230 $6.95 U.S.

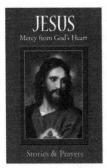

JESUS
Mercy from God's Heart

Written, Compiled, and Edited by
Kathryn J. Hermes, FSP and
Christine Setticase, FSP

Stories from Scripture, true life experiences and prayers from the Christian tradition draw the reader to look at life from a renewed perspective. In these pages you will be challenged to make changes in your life, your way of thinking and your choices. Allow the Lord's unconditional love and limitless mercy to transform your life.

Paperback   144pp.
#40157 $7.95 U.S.

MARY
Help in Hard Times
Compiled and written by
Marianne Lorraine Trouvé, FSP

"Am I not your mother? Do you need anything else?" With these words, Mary was not just speaking to St. Juan Diego, but to the whole world.

As our loving Mother, Mary can help us in all the problems of life:

When illness strikes

When debts pile up

When doubts disturb our faith

When loved ones stray

When the heart seeks solace

Paperback	128 pages
#49391	$7.95 U.S.

BOOKS & MEDIA

A mission of the Daughters of St. Paul

As apostles of Jesus Christ,
evangelizing today's world:

We are CALLED to holiness
by God's living Word and Eucharist.

We COMMUNICATE the Gospel message
through our lives and through all
available forms of media.

We SERVE the Church
by responding to the hopes and needs
of all people with the Word of God,
in the spirit of St. Paul.

For more information visit our website:
www.pauline.org.

BOOKS & MEDIA

The Daughters of St. Paul operate book and media centers at the following addresses. Visit, call or write the one nearest you today, or find us at www.paulinestore.org.

CALIFORNIA
3908 Sepulveda Blvd, Culver City, CA 90230   310-397-8676
3250 Middlefield Road, Menlo Park, CA 94025   650-369-4230

FLORIDA
145 S.W. 107th Avenue, Miami, FL 33174   305-559-6715

HAWAII
1143 Bishop Street, Honolulu, HI 96813   808-521-2731

ILLINOIS
172 North Michigan Avenue, Chicago, IL 60601   312-346-4228

LOUISIANA
4403 Veterans Memorial Blvd, Metairie, LA 70006   504-887-7631

MASSACHUSETTS
885 Providence Hwy, Dedham, MA 02026   781-326-5385

MISSOURI
9804 Watson Road, St. Louis, MO 63126   314-965-3512

NEW YORK
64 W. 38th Street, New York, NY 10018   212-754-1110

SOUTH CAROLINA
243 King Street, Charleston, SC 29401   843-577-0175

TEXAS
Currently no book center; for parish exhibits or outreach evangelization, contact: 210-569-0500, or SanAntonio@paulinemedia.com, or P.O. Box 761416, San Antonio, TX 78245

VIRGINIA
1025 King Street, Alexandria, VA 22314   703-549-3806

CANADA
3022 Dufferin Street, Toronto, ON M6B 3T5   416-781-9131